P9-DHS-196

Little Seeds
of
HOPE

Little Seeds of HOPE

KAREN MOORE

ROYAL·VALUE
PUBLISHING

ROYAL.VALUE
PUBLISHING

© 2014 by Thomas Nelson.

All rights reserved. No portion of this book may be reproduced, stored in a retrieval system, or transmitted in any form or by any means—electronic, mechanical, photocopy, recording, scanning, or other—except for brief quotations in critical reviews or articles, without the prior written permission of the publisher.

Published in Nashville, Tennessee, by Thomas Nelson. Royal Value Publishing is an imprint of Thomas Nelson. Thomas Nelson is a registered trademark of HarperCollins Christian Publishing, Inc.

Unless otherwise noted, Scripture quotations are taken from the New King James Version®. © 1982 by Thomas Nelson, Inc. Used by Permission. All rights reserved.

Scripture quotations marked (NKJV) are taken from the New King James Version®. Copyright © 1982 by Thomas Nelson, Inc. Used by permission. All rights reserved.

Scripture quotations marked (NLT) are taken from the Holy Bible, New Living Translation, copyright © 1996, 2004, 2007 by Tyndale House Foundation. Used by permission of Tyndale House Publishers, Inc., Carol Stream, Illinois 60188. All rights reserved.

Scripture quotations marked (HCSB) are taken from the Holman Christian Standard Bible®, Copyright © 1999, 2000, 2002, 2003 by Holman Bible Publishers. Used by permission.

Scripture marked (NCV) are taken from the New Century Version®. Copyright © 2005 by Thomas Nelson, Inc. Used by permission. All rights reserved.

Scripture quotations marked (MSG) are from THE MESSAGE. Copyright © by Eugene H. Peterson 1993, 1994, 1995, 1996, 2000, 2001, 2002. Used by permission of NavPress Publishing Group.

Library of Congress Cataloging-in-Publication Data

ISBN 978-1-4003-2412-5

Printed in the United States of America

1 2 3 4 5-BTY-18 17 16 15 14

Table of Contents

Introduction:

> Everything that is done in the world is done by hope. No gardener would sow a grain of corn if he hoped not it would grow up and become seed.
>
> *Martin Luther (adapted)*

Most of us live in this world, not just from day to day, nor from event to event, but from hope to hope. In God's grace, we have every reason to hope and every reason to believe that the God of this Universe sees us and knows us and works with us for our good.

There are moments when we experience His mercy and hope almost miraculously! We are awed by His Presence in ways that cause us to respond in humble gratitude. We recognize that He planted a seed of hope within us, a sense of Divine possibility for all we might experience even before we were born.

Sometimes hope sits quietly by, resting on fertile soil, awaiting our hearts to beckon it to bloom. Other times, we dig deeper, praying with all we have for the evidence of things we desire, but cannot yet see. We are assured though that God knows our every need, and that the Master Gardener Himself walks with us through the day.

Little Seeds of Hope are planted everywhere, ready to grow and blossom each time we recognize their gracious presence. They are nourished each time we share their joy. We are the children of God's promise, the recipients of His great Hope. Help yourself to more seeds of His hope and joy through these pages and then dig in and plant new seeds of hope for others. When you do, your joy will be full.

Blessings to you! You have every reason to live in Hope.

—Karen Moore

SECTION ONE:

When Life Falls Apart

❧

For I know the plans I have for you," says the Lord. "They are
plans for good and not for disaster, to give you a future
and a hope."
Jeremiah 29:11 NLT

Prayer of Hope for Today

Father in Heaven, when our hope is gone, we feel like sheep left to wander alone in a world full of wolves. We can no longer muster the courage to try again or to seek the vast possibilities you would put before us. Help all those who have lost their dreams or their careers. Renew the spirits of those who are uncertain or who wonder what is yet possible for their lives. Strengthen each one of them with seeds of hope, planted deeply within their hearts.

AMEN

One: *Vanishing Dreams*

> Most people never run far enough on their first wind to find out they've got a second. Give your dreams all you've got and you'll be amazed at the energy that comes out of you.
>
> *William James*

We like nothing better than to be inspired by new opportunities, courageous dreams, or those seeds of desire planted in our hearts by a loving God. Sometimes those dreams fall quickly into place and we're blessed by each step we take. We feel like nothing can stop us now as our dreams become stronger, blossoming before our eyes. We make the effort and the dream comes to life. We're pleased and gratified.

Other times, as quickly as those dreams take root, they begin to wither and die. As in the Bible story of Jonah who was trying to bask in the shade of a tender plant, only to have it wither and die, we find ourselves unprotected as the dream simply vanishes. Perhaps we shared our dream with others and they couldn't catch the vision or they pruned our optimism and hope back so far, we felt lost and uncertain. We need a second wind. We need to plant our feet firmly in faith. Rest in the assurance of the Lord, who knows exactly where you want to go and will continue to help you get there according to His will and purpose for your life.

Rest in God's love.

We also have joy with our troubles, because we know that these troubles produce patience. And patience produces character, and character produces hope. And this hope will never disappoint us, because God has poured out his love to fill our hearts. He gave us his love through the Holy Spirit, whom God has given to us.

Romans 5: 3-5 NCV

I wait for the Lord; I wait, and put my hope in His word.

Psalm 130: 5 HCSB

God's gifts put man's best dreams to shame.

Elizabeth Barrett Browning

There are many ways of breaking a heart. Stories are full of hearts broken by love, but what really broke a heart was taking away its dream, whatever that dream might be.

Pearl Buck

Dreams do come true, if only we wish hard enough. You can have anything in life if you will sacrifice everything else for it. "What will you have?" says God. "Pray for it and take it."

James M. Barrie

Hope and a Prayer

Lord, you are the true author of dreams. Thank you for blessing my life with goals to strive for and dreams to pursue. Help me to be patient when things fall apart, trusting in you for all that I am and all that is yet to be. In the name of Jesus, I pray.

AMEN

Two: *Careers in Crisis and Clipped Wings*

> A person's character and their garden both reflect the amount of weeding that was done in the growing season.
>
> *Author Unknown*

Having any kind of sustainable career these days requires more than talent. It requires an unprecedented willingness to change, to have your wings clipped just when you thought you would soar and to trust God's plan for your life. You probably trained for your life work, going to college or working hard at a job and those things shaped your direction. You made choices and hoped to succeed.

The fact is that careers change and the path you thought you would walk when you first started out, changes too. It turns out that very few people actually work in the field they trained for at the beginning. Of course, that may be small comfort when you're hoping to rise to a certain level in your chosen career. What happens then, when you've worked hard for a promotion, only to be passed over by someone you didn't even see coming?

A career change or disappointment often happens unexpectedly. It can feel like the rug was pulled out from beneath your feet. It may cause you to wonder if there's anything more to hope for as your dreams disappear.

Let your hope rest in the promise of God who has a plan and a purpose for your life. Have the courage to begin a change, perhaps not in your specific career choice, but in your perception of it.

Your life purpose is a beautiful plant in a garden of opportunity. If you're uprooted along the way, it's simply to give you the chance to find more fertile soil for the things you've been created to do. Trust in the seeds of hope planted and set to bloom in you. Trust in what God has already done to prepare the way for you to start again.

We are pressed on every side by troubles, but we are not crushed and broken. We are perplexed, but we don't give up and quit. We are hunted down, but God never abandons us. We get knocked down, but we get up again and keep going.

2 Corinthians 4:8-9 NLT

It's the diligent farmer who gets the produce.

2 Timothy 2:6 The Message

Commit your works to the Lord, and your thoughts will be established.

Proverbs 16:3 NKJV

In all the work you are doing, work the best you can. Work as if you were doing it for the Lord, not for people.

Colossians 3:23 NCV

I long to accomplish a great and noble task; but it is my chief duty to accomplish small tasks as if they were great and noble.

Helen Keller

If a man is called a street-sweeper, he should sweep streets even as Michelangelo painted, or Beethoven composed music, or Shakespeare wrote poetry. He should sweep streets so well that all the hosts of heaven and earth will pause to say, "Here lived a great street-sweeper who did his job well."

George Smith Patton

Far and away the best prize that life offers is the chance to work hard at work worth doing.

Theodore Roosevelt

In perplexities--when we cannot tell what to do, when we cannot understand what is going on around us—let us be calmed and steadied and made patient by the thought that what is hidden from us is not hidden from Him.

Frances Ridley Havergal

'Tis the lesson you should heed,
Try, try again.
If at first you don't succeed,
Try, try again.

William Edward Hickson

Hope and a Prayer

Dear Lord, help me to know the purpose for my
life so I put all my effort into meaningful work.
As my career changes and the path becomes
uncertain, light the way and lead me to more
fertile ground. Help me to discover more of the
gifts you've given me so that I might use them to
your glory. Thank you for your faithfulness, for
that alone gives me real hope.

AMEN

Three: *Uprooted Again… Those Unexpected Moves!*

This is the true nature of home—it is the place of peace; the shelter, not only from injury, but from all terror, doubt and division.

John Ruskin

The very thought of leaving home and moving, being uprooted, going to a new city or a new job or another country makes most of us want to run away. More than packing up, we're wondering if we can pack it in. Yet, we know change is inevitable. We've been around long enough to know that life is all about change and change seeks an attitude of hope.

So what do we do when we're more tempted to act like resistant weeds in a garden than those who trust in God to create opportunities for us to blossom elsewhere? We set our minds on those things that create hope.

Moving anywhere and for any reason, even good reasons, can cause your spirits to wilt. If you're familiar with the Genesis story of Abraham in the Bible, you probably remember how the Lord sent him and his family to a whole different country, to a place Abraham had never been before. Abraham probably didn't know what to think about that move. He may not even have been excited to pack up his tents and his servants and his family and head out to the desert, but he did it. He did it because he had hope. Abraham knew that God was with him wherever he went and that he could not move away from God. God would go before him and prepare just the right place for him to relocate. Abraham had hope in God, and you can too.

If you're moving out, moving on or simply moving around, know that you have hope because God will go with you. He promises to always be by your side, to never leave you wandering alone. He'll help you set down new roots. You can count on Him with every box you pack. He's already preparing new soil and new seeds to help your grow.

It was by faith that Abraham obeyed when God called him to leave home and go to another land that God would give him as his inheritance. He went without knowing where he was going. And even when he reached the land God promised him, he lived there by faith—for he was like a foreigner, living in a tent. And so did Isaac and Jacob, to whom God gave the same promise. Abraham did this because he was confidently looking forward to a city with eternal foundations, a city designed and built by God.

Hebrews 11:8-10 NLT

How can we sing the Lord's song in a foreign land?

Psalm 137:4 NKJV

The God who laid out earth on ocean foundations,
   His love never quits.
The God who filled the skies with light,
   His love never quits.
The sun to watch over the day,
   His love never quits.
Moon and stars as guardians of the night,
   His love never quits.

Psalm 136:6-9 The Message

Give your entire attention to what God is doing right now, and don't get worked up about what may or may not happen tomorrow. God will help you deal with whatever hard things come up when the time comes.

Matthew 6:34 The Message

The bend in the road is not the end of the road, unless you fail to make the turn.

Unknown author

Most of the important things in the world have been accomplished by people who have kept trying when there seemed to be no hope at all.

Dale Carnegie

Experience is not what happens to you, it is what you do with what happens to you.

Aldous Huxley (adapted)

The smallest seed of faith is better than the largest fruit of happiness.

Henry David Thoreau

I really learned to practice mustard seed faith, and positive thinking, and remarkable things happened.

Sir John Walton

We love to expect good things, and when expectation is either disappointed or gratified, we want to begin again expecting good things.

Samuel Johnson (adapted)

Hope and a Prayer

Dear Lord, thank you for watching over me as I work through some unexpected changes. Thank you for preparing new opportunities and giving me hope even when the path looks uncertain and my plans are shaken. Help me to trust that all is well and that together we'll find a way to bring peace back to my life again. Even though I feel like I'm standing in the weeds, I look for the buds of hope that are not yet in my view.

AMEN

Four: *Growing in the Wild...those Fears and Uncertainties!*

What we fear comes to pass more speedily than what we hope.
Syrus

When the circumstances of life change and we're forced to change with it, we can wonder what it all means, wonder if things will ever feel comfortable and safe again. We might feel like everything has gone wild or like nothing makes sense and so worry and uncertainty prevail.

If you can, step back a little and think about times you've been in this situation before. Perhaps you were a child and had to sing a solo at church. You loved to sing but didn't feel confident that you could sing in front of other people. Fear set in. Most likely though, you overcame the fear and sang your heart out. Perhaps someone encouraged you, gave you hope and helped you work through the fear.

As an adult, that fear of the unknown has probably happened to you a number of times. Maybe you had dreams for a certain career path, but your family situation made it difficult for you to follow your dreams. You made other choices for the good of others, fearful that you might never have your own dreams realized.

The beauty of looking back is that you can see that you got through whatever your difficult or changing circumstances may have been and that someone was there who planted a seed of hope in you at the time. That hope proved to make your circumstance easier to deal with and looking back, you can see God's hand in what happened. You can see that going through the circumstance created other positive opportunities in your life.

You may feel like you're alone sometimes, growing like a wild weed in the middle of a prairie, but the truth is, you are always known, always guided, always surrounded with the hope that helps you enjoy the sunshine again. God wants you to thrive in any circumstance as you put your hope in Him!

Don't be afraid, because the Lord your God will be with you everywhere you go.

Joshua 1:9 NCV

Therefore, humble yourselves under the mighty hand of God, that He may exalt you in due time, casting all your care upon Him, for He cares for you.

1 Peter 5:7 NKJV

When the clouds are full of water, it rains. When the wind blows down a tree, it lies where it falls. Don't sit there watching the wind. Do your own work. Don't stare at the clouds. Get on with your life.

Ecclesiastes 11:3-4 The Message

Those who plant in tears will harvest with shouts of joy. They weep as they go to plant their seed, but they sing as they return with the harvest.

Psalm 126:5-6 NLT

We were saved, and we have this hope. If we see what we are waiting for, that is not really hope. People do not hope for something they already have. But we are hoping for something we do not have yet, and we are waiting for it patiently.

Romans 8:24-25 NCV

We gain strength, and courage, and confidence by each experience in which we really stop to look fear in the face…we must do that which we think we cannot.

Eleanor Roosevelt

Don't fear change, embrace it.

Anthony J. D'Angelo

Prosperity is not without many fears and distastes; and adversity is not without comforts and hopes.

Francis Bacon

As aromatic plants bestow
No spicy fragrance while they grow;
But crushed or trodden to the ground,
Diffuse their balmy sweets around.

Oliver Goldsmith

Adversity is like the period of the rain... cold, comfortless, unfriendly to human or animal; yet from that season have their birth the flower, the fruit, the date, the rose and the pomegranate.

Sir Walter Scott

With malice toward none; with charity for all; with firmness in the right, as God give us to see the right—let us strive to finish the work we are in.

Abraham Lincoln

Courage faces fear and thereby masters it. Cowardice represses fear and is thereby mastered by it.

Martin Luther King

Hope and a Prayer

Dear Lord, when life seems scary, please come closer to me. Help me to recognize that change and uncertainty are not matters to be faced alone, but to be faced with hope and with trust in you. Shine your light on the circumstances of my life and help me to be patient, letting go of fear and embracing the opportunity to grow stronger in character and in joy. I will move forward in hope, believing that good things will come from what I'm experiencing now.

AMEN

Five: *Parched and Dry:* *Thirsty for Hope*

God can do wonders with a broken heart; if we give him all the pieces.

Unknown author

Victor Frankl said that the last of the human freedoms was to be able to choose one's attitude in any given set of circumstances, to choose one's own way.

The fact is that as human beings we don't always make wise choices. We sometimes choose too hastily or with the wrong motive. We sometimes choose not to choose and then consequences still haunt us for our indecision.

When life falls apart, it's primarily due to our unfortunate choices, the ones we regret in some measure, the ones that leave us parched and dry. The problem of choices is that sometimes you have too many and no path seems clearly marked. Other times you feel as if you have no choice at all and so you move begrudgingly into the circumstance, resisting all possibility for a positive outcome.

God gave us free will so that we could make wise choices. He gave us guidance through His Word and His Spirit. He gives us friends and family to be our counselors and encouragers when we can't determine a course for ourselves.

The beautiful thing about choice though is that it flows like a river. There are always other choices that can be made, more options to be discovered. When you feel like you've made poor choices, ask God to help you and choose again. You do not have to be stuck in a dry desert. You can always find the hope that comes from Living Water.

I will give free water from the spring of the water of life to anyone who is thirsty. Those who win the victory will receive this, and I will be their God, and they will be my children.

Revelation 21:6-7 NCV

Hey there! All who are thirsty, come to the water! Are you penniless? Come anyway—buy and eat! Come buy your drinks, buy wine and milk. Buy without money—everything's free!

Isaiah 55:1 The Message

"If you only knew the gift God has for you and who I am, you would ask me, and I would give you living water."

JESUS

John 4:10 NLT

"Whoever drinks of this water will thirst again, but whoever drinks of the water that I shall give him will never thirst. But the water that I shall give him will become in him a fountain of water springing up into everlasting life."

JESUS

John 4:13-14 NKJV

The strongest principle of growth lies in the human choice.

George Eliot

Spiritual growth consists most in the growth of the root, which is out of sight.

Matthew Henry

Making choices means…

> Choosing to love, rather than fear.
>
> Choosing to smile, rather than frown.
>
> Choosing to build up, rather than tear down.
>
> Choosing to persevere, rather than quit.
>
> Choosing kind words, rather than gossip.
>
> Choosing to heal, rather than wound.
>
> Choosing to give, rather than take.
>
> Choosing to act, rather than ignore.
>
> Choosing to forgive, rather than grow bitter.
>
> Choosing to pray, rather than despair.

How will you choose to live your day today?

Hope and a Prayer

Lord, you know I've made some pretty foolish choices. I have gone dry sometimes, not remembering that you are near ready to give me the living water of your joy and hope. Help me to come to you sooner rather than later when I'm lost or broken. Help me to look for you in all the choices that I make and seek your guidance and clarity. Help me to trust my life to your grace and mercy.

Amen

Section Two:

Sowing the Good Seed of Relationships

Watch what God does, and then you do it, like children who learn proper behavior from their parents. Mostly what God does is love you. Keep company with him and learn a life of love. Observe how Christ loved us. His love was not cautious but extravagant. He didn't love in order to get something from us but to give everything of himself to us. Love like that.

Ephesians 5:1-2 The Message

Prayer of Hope
for Today

Lord, you have taught us that life is about
relationship. You made it possible for human
beings to communicate with you and you
have provided us with examples of what good
relationships look like through your Word. The
hope of the world lies in our abilities to learn
to love and to help each other become all we're
meant to be. All we know about love we have
learned from you. Help us to share the light, the
joy, and the hope of authentic and lasting love
with one another.

AMEN

One: A Heart Full of Hope and Promise

> The greatest happiness of life is the conviction that we are loved—loved for ourselves or rather, loved in spite of ourselves.
>
> *Victor Hugo*

Probably nothing puts more hope in a heart or spring in a step, like love. When we meet someone special, we begin to smile for no reason at all, begin to see the world with more color and beauty, and begin to hope in the goodness of life in ways we never really did before. Yes, love is a beautiful thing!

So, why does a love relationship need an infusion of hope? What causes us to flounder so that love grows cold and distant or is even lost? Love is about connection and it's about relationship. God serves as our best example of what it can be in its ultimate form. We who are designed in God's image, are designed for love, and meant to be in relationship with one another.

Whether your love relationship is new, or whether you've enjoyed it for many years, love always carries a message of hope. It's the eternal gift of happiness, the thing that keeps you wanting to wake up each morning. When the connection is lost or changed, your heart can despair.

God offers the hope of new possibility. He offers grace and forgiveness and mercy for moments when painful words or actions have entered in. If love exists in spite of us, then we have to give it every opportunity to blossom and grow and become stronger. We have to nurture it and keep it fresh so it can thrive and continue to be the light of our lives. May your love for each other be covered over in hope and happiness.

Above all else, guard your heart, for it affects everything you do.

Proverbs 4:23 NLT

Be happy with the wife you married when you were young. She gives you joy, as your fountain gives you water. She is as lovely and graceful as a deer. Let her love always make you happy, let her love always hold you captive.

Proverbs 5:18-19 NCV

It's your heart, not the dictionary that gives meaning to your words. A good person produces good deeds and words season after season.

Matthew 12:34-35 The Message

Don't just pretend that you love others. Really love them. Hate what is wrong. Stand on the side of the good. Love each other with genuine affection, and take delight in honoring each other.

Romans 12:9-10 NLT

We are each of us angels with only one wing,
And we can only fly embracing each other.

Luciano De Creschenzo

To handle yourself, use your head. To handle others, use your heart.

Author unknown

Courage is like love; it must have hope for nourishment.

Napoleon

When you say a situation or a person is hopeless, you are slamming the door in the face of God.

Charles Allen

Where there is love, there is a trinity;
a lover, a beloved and a spring of love.

Augustine of Hippo

Hope and a Prayer

Lord, restore to all those who love, a sense of peace and affection. Bless the relationships that may have suffered painful events or harsh words. Offer new seeds of hope into the hearts of those who wonder if love will ever blossom for them again. You have designed us for love so that we may open our hearts to each other and to you in every possible way. Grant that all relationships built on love would become evergreen and ever strong.

AMEN

Two: *Strengthening the Family Tree*

> God designed the family to be a spiritual garden that grows flowers for today and seeds for tomorrow.
>
> *Dennis and Barbara Rainey*

You may wonder sometimes how a nice person like you got into the family you have. You've got a few favorite aunts or a delightful grandmother, but where did you get Uncle Moe or Cousin Earl? Somehow, they don't seem to fit, but you're all family, so what can you do?

What are some ways that you can help your family thrive? We're not talking about just your immediate family, though that's important, we're talking about the family as a whole, the ones from your family tree. Perhaps you're even interested in your family heritage, researching your genealogy so that you can know more about your family roots.

A family thrives by showing each other you care and that you recognize and value your connection. Seeds of hope may blossom all around you as you try some of these ideas:

- Pray for each other. That may mean to remember your grandma who is traveling in Europe, or to offer prayers for new babies, or teenagers in crisis, or prayers for peace in each family household.

- Communicate. Keep in touch with your family members on Facebook or on emails or by picking up the phone and calling. If you don't feel like you know a particular family member very well, take the time to get to know them. Your connection to them may be just the ray of hope they need.

- Get Together. Make plans to share fun times together and take opportunities to grow the bonds you have as family. Play board games or rent your favorite movies.

- Laugh. Find times to simply enjoy telling stories about your lives, sharing fun moments and little tidbits that you might not know about each other.

- Honor. Be sure to honor each other, even when you don't agree with each other's actions or ideas. Extend grace to one another in all ways. Nurture and encourage each other's spirits.

Yes, family relationships can sometimes feel hopeless or confusing. They can leave you wondering what you have in common beyond DNA. The fact is, God put you all together for a reason. See if you can discover just what He had in mind. May your family grow in joy today and in hope for tomorrow!

Wives, understand and support your husbands by submitting to them in ways that honor the Master. Husbands, go all out in love for your wives. Don't take advantage of them. Children do what your parents tell you. This delights the Master to no end. Parents, don't come down too hard on your children or you'll crush their spirits.

Colossians 3:18-21 The Message

All the families of the earth will be blessed through you and your descendants. I am with you and will protect you everywhere you go and will bring you back to this land. I will not leave you until I have done what I have promised you.

Genesis 28:14-15 NCV

God places the lonely in families.

Psalm 68:6 NLT

The family was ordained by God before he established any other institution, even before he established the church.

Billy Graham

Family life is too intimate to be preserved by the spirit of justice. It can be sustained by a spirit of love which goes beyond justice.

Reinhold Niebuhr

All happy families are like one another; each unhappy family is unhappy in its own way.

Tolstoy

Hope is not the conviction that something will turn out well, but the certainty that something makes sense, regardless of how it turns out.

Vaclav Havel

Hope and a Prayer

Lord, thank you for my family. Thank you for the ones who inspire my thinking and who encourage my way. Thank you for the ones that need my help and support. Thank you even for the ones I don't understand well, who cause me to apply grace and kindness to any interactions I have with them. Lord, build us up as a family. Grant that we might plant seeds of joy for each other and bring peace and hope to each of our homes.

AMEN

Three: Of Toddlers, Teens, and In-Betweens

We can't form our children on our own concepts; we must take them and love them as God gives them to us.

Goethe

When babies are born to us, it's like the hope of the world has just been placed in our care. Here is the child we prayed for and longed to love. Here is the possibility for new dreams to come true. Of course, along the way there are times when it's not so much fun to be a parent to a toddler, or a budding teen, but we're in it for the long haul. God knew when we started, we'd see this project through, doing our best to be gracious guides.

Each stage and age of our children brings an unspeakable gift, an opportunity to be blessed beyond measure. Here is a toddler, who places every need and every confidence in the parents that feed and hold him. Here are the parents who are in awe of what God can do through the love of a little child. Hope reigns.

That in-between stage, where your little seedling, is not quite a blossom, but a healthy growing, leggy stem, brings its own rewards and challenges. Too much light or water, and they begin to fade. Too little attention and they don't get the proper nourishment. This is the age of reason and no reason. This is the stage where steadfast and faithful parenting is the name of the game. Here is where your tender sprout learns to cope with the ups and downs of life.

Hope prevails as teenagers begin to discover paths for themselves. They've enjoyed a safe exploration within your care up till now, but soon they will branch out and perhaps set down roots somewhere else. They need growing room and they need your prayers. More than anything they need to know that the hope you had on the day they were born is still there, stronger than ever! Your teens and your adult children need to know that you see them as the hope of the future wherever life takes them. It seems certain God does!

Point your kids in the right direction—when they're old they won't be lost.

Proverbs 22:6 The Message

Young people are prone to foolishness and fads; the cure comes through tough-minded discipline.

> Proverbs 22:15 The Message

Children are a gift from the Lord; they are a reward from him.

> Psalm 127:3 NLT

Correct your children while there is still hope; do not let them destroy themselves.

> Proverbs 19:18 NCV

The family should be a place where each new human being can have an early atmosphere conducive to the development of constructive creativity.

> Edith Schaeffer

Children are our most valuable natural resource.

> Herbert Hoover

The potential possibilities of any child are the most intriguing and stimulating in all creation.

> Ray. L. Wilbur

Children today are tyrants. They contradict their parents, gobble their food and tyrannize their teachers.

Socrates

Perhaps there is no more important component of character than steadfast resolution. The boys and girls who are going to make great men and women, or are going to count in any way, must make up their minds not merely to overcome a thousand obstacles, but to win in spite of a thousand repulses and defeats.

Theodore Roosevelt

The mind of Christ is to be learned in the family. Strength of character may be acquired at work, but beauty of character is learned at home. There the affections are trained.

Henry Drummond

Hope and a Prayer

Lord, thank you for the gift of children. Thank you that in each phase of their lives, we learn more about what it means to be parents. Thank you that you guide us and help us to do our job well so that our children become what you dreamed they might be. Bless the children of the world for they are the hope of the world. Help us all to parent any child who comes into our lives with love.

AMEN

Four: *Friends for All Seasons*

> The glory of friendship is not the outstretched hand, nor the kindly smile, nor the joy of companionship; it is the spiritual inspiration that comes to one when he discovers that someone else believes in him and is willing to trust him with his friendship.
>
> *Ralph Waldo Emerson*

If family is the way we establish our roots on earth's soil, then friends are the fertilizer. Friends are the sunshine and the rain, the ones who help us grow to be better and stronger than we'd be on our own. In that regard we cultivate a variety of types of friends.

Some friends are part of our work environment and they bring us insight into the projects at hand or the opportunities around us. They nurture our desires to become better at the things we do. They encourage our growth along the path of our career choices.

Some friends are part of our church life. We see them on Sundays and catch up with them about life's everyday events, serve on committees with them, and spend time at retreats. They support our faith and offer insights into our beliefs. They sprinkle seeds of hope into our lives and bless our days.

Then, if we're truly blessed, there's a friend or two, who creates a space for us like no one else can do. They help us to dig deeper into who we are and what we want out of life. They nourish our spirits with laughter and warm conversations each time we meet. They see us as we are and offer whatever we need from shelter in a storm, to sunshine when the clouds roll in. They are the gifts that truly strengthen our growth and help us become beautiful.

These friends are with you when hope is thin, the ones who remind you brighter days are just ahead and that God is with you. This kind of friendship is rooted in love.

A friend is always loyal, and a brother is born to help in time of need.

Proverbs 17:17 NLT

A real friend sticks closer than a brother.

Proverbs 18:24 NLT

Overlook an offense and bond a friendship, fasten on to a slight and — goodbye, friend!

Proverbs 17:9 The Message

Observe people who are good at their work — skilled workers are always in demand and admired; they don't take a backseat to anyone.

Proverbs 22:29 The Message

Do not forsake your own friend or your father's friend.

Proverbs 27:10 NKJV

The more we love, the better we are, and the greater our friendships are, the dearer we are to God.

Jeremy Taylor

True friendship is a plant of slow growth, and must undergo and withstand the shocks of adversity before it is entitled to the name of "friend."

George Washington (adapted)

Sometimes being a friend means mastering the art of timing. There is a time for silence. A time to let go and allow people to hurl themselves into their own destiny. And a time to prepare to pick up the pieces when it's all over.

Octavia Butler

Sometimes our light goes out but is blown into flame by another human being. Each of us owes deepest thanks to those who have rekindled this light.

Albert Schweitzer

Hope and a Prayer

Lord, you bless us with people who come into our lives at the right moments and some of them plant seeds of love in our hearts that grow throughout our lifetime. Thank you for those friends who nurture us and help us to dig deeper within ourselves to become more than we ever dreamed we might be. Thank you too for those friends who are part of our work or our church or who offer us hope in every area of life.

AMEN

Five: Next Door Neighbors and Garden Gates

> The race of mankind would perish did they cease to aid each other. We cannot exist without mutual help. All therefore that need aid have a right to ask for it from their fellow man; and no one who has the power of granting can refuse it without guilt.
>
> *Sir Walter Scott*

Some of us grew up in neighborhoods. We knew most of the people that lived on our street or in the houses surrounding ours. As neighbors, we knew we could count on each other when times were tough and that we all had a lot in common.

It's not quite so easy to define neighbors today. Sure, neighborhoods still exist, but the advent of the internet has changed our definition of "neighbor" in a way that nothing before it has done. Now we realize that we have "neighbors" who live in other states that need our help when hurricanes and tornados level their homes. We see that there are children starving in countries around the globe and there's a strong realization that we're part of a bigger neighborhood, a huge global family, and we each have a part in that family as well. Seeds of hope need to be planted in the hearts and homes of people close to us, but sometimes, our neighbors are far away. Those who reach across a television screen or computer monitor asking for our prayers are seeking hope.

A 17th century proverb says, "Good fences make good neighbors." Perhaps so! Sometimes we need to keep boundaries, but hope is something that must be offered in community. It asks us to share what we have and who we are. It causes us to plant new seeds of possibility.

It's great to have good neighbors. When God reminded us to "love our neighbors," He had a wide net. He knew our neighborhoods would expand to the same measure as our hearts were willing to give. Love your neighbor, offer hope to those in need, and your life will be forever rooted in joy.

It is good and pleasant when God's people live together in peace!

Psalm 133:1 NCV

Love your neighbor as you love yourself.

Matthew 19:19 NCV

The Samaritan

"There was once a man traveling from Jerusalem to Jericho. On the way he was attacked by robbers. They took his clothes, beat him up, and went off leaving him half-dead. Luckily, a priest was on his way down the same road, but when he saw him he angled across to the other side. Then a Levite religious man showed up; he also avoided the injured man.

A Samaritan traveling the road came on to him. When he saw the man's condition, his heart went out to him. He gave him first aid, disinfecting and bandaging his wounds. Then he lifted him onto his donkey, led him to an inn, and made him comfortable. In the morning he took out two silver coins and gave them to the innkeeper, saying, "Take good care of him. If it costs any more, put it on my bill—I'll pay you on my way back."

"What do you think? Which of the three became a neighbor to the man attacked by robbers?"

"The one who treated him kindly," the religion scholar responded.

Jesus said, "Go and do the same."

Luke 10:30-37 The Message

There is no principle of the heart that is more acceptable to God than a universal, ardent love for all mankind, which seeks and prays for their happiness.

William Law

The love of God is the first and great commandment. But love for our neighbor is the means by which we obey it. Since we cannot see God directly, God allows us to catch sight of him through our neighbor. By loving our neighbor we purge our eyes to see God. So love your neighbor and you will discover that in doing so you come to know God.

Augustine of Hippo

Do not waste your time bothering about whether you love your neighbor; act as if you did...When you are behaving as if you love someone, you will presently come to love him.

C.S.Lewis

He alone loves the Creator perfectly
who manifests a pure love for his neighbor.

Bede

There are no ordinary people.

C.S.Lewis

We cannot live only for ourselves! A thousand fibers connect us with our fellow men and women!

Herman Melville (adapted)

Hope and a Prayer

Lord, you taught us that we should treat others the way we want to be treated. If we want good friends and neighbors, we should be good friends and neighbors. Help us to be your hope, your hands and feet, and your light in our own neighborhoods, or in any sphere of influence we may have. Grant that we might see our neighborhood as your garden, a place where each kind gesture becomes a freshly planted seed of hope.

AMEN

SECTION THREE:

Comfort for You When Things Feel Hopeless!

"Don't be afraid, I've redeemed you. I've called your name. You're mine. When you're in over your head, I'll be there with you. When you're in rough waters, you will not go down. When you're between a rock and a hard place, it won't be a dead end."

Isaiah 43:2 The Message

Prayer of Hope
for Today

Lord, we often go through rough waters, times
when the losses feel greater than the wins. We
come to you for comfort and peace and mercy.
We look to you to protect our hearts and minds
when we are most vulnerable. Help everyone
today who suffers the loss of someone close to
them, who is stunned over the loss of a job, or
who simply grieve the loss of a life ambition. Let
us draw near to you, as broken as we are, and rest
in the comfort of your wings.

Amen

One: *Which Way Was I Going?*

In the book of life, the answers aren't in the back.

Charlie Brown

When you were a kid, you may have dreamed about what you'd be when you grew up. At five, you pictured yourself as a superhero or a cowgirl. When you were fifteen, you might have imagined being a baseball player or a drum major leading the band. Ultimately, you began a vocation after high school or college and thought you might have that job as a career for the rest of your life.

The problem is the rest of your life may change quickly if the company you worked for goes out of business, or new technology means your job is no longer necessary. Everything you know can be lost in that one event.

Devastating things happen in life and leave you feeling hopeless! Illness wipes out the ability to work. A car accident leaves you distraught. A tornado destroys your home and business. Unexpected events shake every foundation and your trust in the goodness of life is strained. You're suddenly set adrift, with nowhere to go and nowhere you want to go. You imagine the system has failed you or that God has left you.

Whatever the circumstances that bring a loss of your life direction, there is still reason to maintain a sense of hope. This kind of hope is built on trust, not in yourself or others, but in your Creator. Your hope rests on the awareness that God is in control. God calls you by your first name and knows the number of hairs on your head, knows you intimately. He holds you up and has a plan for your life. He has your present and your future in His hands. Take comfort in that knowledge. He will plant new seeds of hope in your heart. Trust him!

I leave you peace; my peace I give you. I do not give it to you as the world does. So don't let your hearts be troubled or afraid.

John 14:27 NCV

We throw open our doors to God and discover at the same moment that he has already thrown open his door to us. We find ourselves standing where we always hoped we might stand—out in the wide open spaces of God's grace and glory, standing tall and shouting our praise. There's more to come: We continue to shout our praise even when we're hemmed in with troubles, because we know how troubles can develop passionate patience in us, and how that patience in turn forges the tempered steel of virtue, keeping us alert for whatever God will do next. In alert expectancy such as this, we're never left feeling shortchanged.

Romans 5:2-4 The Message

Two sparrows cost only a penny, but not even one of them can die without your Father's knowing it. God even knows how many hairs are on your head. So don't be afraid. You are worth much more than many sparrows.

Matthew 10:29-31 NCV

The game of life is not so much in holding a good hand as in playing a poor hand well.

H.T.Leslie

It is impossible for men and women to despair when we remember our Helper is omnipotent.

Jeremy Taylor (adapted)

Don't ask for an easier life; ask to be a stronger person. Sometimes you just have to take the leap, and build your wings on the way down.

Yamada

The life of an individual only has meaning insofar as it aids in making the life of every living thing nobler and more beautiful. Life is sacred, that is to say, it is the supreme value to which all other values are subordinate.

Albert Einstein

Hope and a Prayer

Lord, it's not easy to have the bottom fall out of all the plans I made. I thought I was headed in a good direction and now I'm not sure I have any sense of direction at all. As I stand here, almost in mid-air wondering if I'll land in a safe place again, I can do nothing more than count on you. I ask you to be my safety net. Please help me grow through this process and comfort me and all those who suffer a change in the direction they thought life would go. Help us all to be strong.

AMEN

Two: The Grief beyond Measure

Peace does not mean the end of all our striving
Joy does not mean the drying of our tears.
Peace is the power that comes to souls arriving
Up to the light where God Himself appears.

Geoffrey A.S. Kennedy

Nothing strikes the heart so deeply as losing someone we have dearly loved. Since God designed us to be happiest in relationship with Him and with each other, grief over such a loss is appropriate and understandable. What comfort can we find when our hearts are breaking? What solace can there be when those closest to us move on to Heaven's gate?

Our faith gives us one possibility. We can hope in the day when we'll all meet again, when we too go home to our Lord. Trusting in that, we can imagine that glorious day when we'll meet each other with hugs of joy and embrace our new life together in the place that has no more tears.

For now though, friends and neighbors bring us their comforting hugs and their truly hopeful wishes for brighter days ahead. They remind us to hold our memories of our loved one in the scrapbook of our minds, taking the special moments out to look at any time we choose.

However we manage grief, the true hope comes from knowing that even God grieves with us. He sees us right where we are and longs to hold us close and help us through the darkness we feel. He will never leave us alone. He offers us His unending light that will never perish.

Perhaps you could plant a tree in honor of the one you loved. As you tend it and nourish its growth, your love will cause it to blossom into new life, a gentle reminder that love never truly ends even when it's transformed by God's grace and mercy.

The Lord is my shepherd; I have everything I need. He lets me rest in green meadows; he leads me beside peaceful streams. He renews my strength. He guides me along right paths, bringing honor to his name.

Even when I walk through the dark valley of death, I will not be afraid, for you are close beside me. Your rod and your staff protect and comfort me.

You prepare a feast for me in the presence of my enemies. You welcome me as a guest, anointing my head with oil. My cup overflows with blessings.

Surely your goodness and unfailing love will pursue me all the days of my life, and I will live in the house of the Lord forever.

Psalm 23 NLT

As one whom his mother comforts,
So will I comfort you.

Isaiah 66:13 NKJV

For the love of God is broader
Than the measures of man's mind;
And the heart of the Eternal
Is most wonderfully kind.

F. W. Faber

Our ground of hope is that God does not weary of mankind.

Ralph W. Sockman

God loved the world so much that he gave his one and only Son so that whoever believes in him may not be lost, but have eternal life.

John 3:16 NCV

"Don't be troubled. You trust God, now trust in me. There are many rooms in my Father's home, and I am going to prepare a place for you. If this were not so, I would not tell you plainly. When everything is ready, I will come and get you, so that you will always be with me where I am."

John 14:1-3 NLT

Hearts on earth say in the course of a joyful experience, "I don't want this ever to end." But it invariably does. The hearts of those in heaven say, "I want this to go on forever." And it will. There is no better news than this.

J.I.Packer

One day we will meet beside the river and our Lord will dry every tear. For now, we must live in the joy of that promise and recall that for every generation life is hard, but God is faithful.

Bodie Thoene

Hope and a Prayer

Lord, thank you for holding us up in the hour of our grief. Thank you for knowing how painful it is to lose someone we love. We know that there is a cycle of life and no matter how much our minds can grasp the reality of it, our hearts struggle with loss and mourn deeply the absence of those who move on to Heaven. Help us to be comforted by knowing your presence and give us hope in a life eternal.

AMEN

Three: *People, Pets, and Paradise*

Animals are such agreeable friends—they ask no questions, they pass no criticisms.

George Eliot

Pets are some of the most delightful members of a family. They love with full hearts, putting all their trust in those who care for them. They run and play with abandon because they know they are safe in their own domain. They live, in a sense, with the kind of child-like faith that God could only hope for from human beings.

Losing a pet is its own form of pain. Perhaps part of the reason is that a pet which has loved you and been part of your life, never made you feel uncomfortable about who you are. They never asked you to change or be more of what they hoped you might be just for them. They never judged your actions or activities. You lived in a relationship of total acceptance and grace. When you think about it, that's an amazing gift.

It's no wonder that God grieves with you when you lose a pet friend. It's no wonder that He created these amazing companions to give solace, to guide the broken, and to offer a kind of love that can't be had in any other way. Pets are such a cause for celebration and joy.

As you honor the memory of your beloved pet, thank God for all you shared and all you learned from each other. If seeds of hope were ever planted, they surely thrive and grow in the love shared between furry companions and the people who love them. What a blessing to have such an experience!

May you treasure your furry friend forever.

The Lord says, "I am the one who comforts you."
Isaiah 51:12 NCV

May the Lord bless you and protect you,
May the Lord smile on you and be gracious to you.
May the Lord show you his favor and give you his peace.

Numbers 6:24-26 NLT

Give all your worries to him, because he cares about you.

1 Peter 5:7 NCV

Surely we ought to show animals great kindness and gentleness for many reasons, but, above all, because they are of the same origin as ourselves.

John Chrysostom

All animals except man know that the ultimate of life is to enjoy it.

Samuel Butler

If having a soul means being able to feel love and loyalty and gratitude, then animals are better off than a lot of humans.

James Herriot

It is not just that animals make the world more scenic or picturesque. The lives of animals are woven into our very being - closer than our own breathing - and our soul will suffer when they are gone.

Gary Kowalski, Author of *The Souls of Animals*

If there are no dogs in Heaven, then when I die I want to go where they went.

Will Rogers

We must accept finite disappointment, but we must never lose infinite hope.

Martin Luther King

Until he extends his circle of compassion to include all living things, man will not himself find peace.

Albert Schweitzer

Hope and a Prayer

Lord, losing a friend, even a four-footed or winged one, is heartbreaking. You've built into the very nature of loving pets, that sense of assurance and peace that comes from knowing real love. You've created opportunities for greater understanding of what love and loyalty and trust are meant to be in each relationship of a pet with a human caretaker. Bless all those who have lost beloved pets and comfort them with your presence and peace. Welcome all our furry friends into Paradise.

AMEN

Four: *Financial Fumes and Dwindling Dollars*

All the resources of the Godhead are at our disposal!
Jonathan Goforth

If you've been living on financial fumes over the loss of a job or your major source of income, you may struggle with a concept of hope. It's hard to be hopeful when your dollars are dwindling and the bill collectors are pounding on your door. Worry sets in and hope flies out the window.

Though it is natural to worry about our financial difficulties, the Bible reminds us that worry isn't actually much of a benefit. In the Gospel of Matthew we're told to not worry about everyday life, whether we'll have enough of the things that keep life feeling okay like food and clothes and shelter.

If you've been downsized, right-sized, or outsized in one way or another, you may imagine it's your fault somehow. Most likely, it isn't. Job security has become a thing of the past.

Fortunately, you have security in God. He knows you need income. He hears your prayers. He may ask you to seek a whole new direction but He will work to make all things come together for your good. He will go ahead of you to find opportunities to secure your future.

When your resources are tapped out, tap into God's wisdom and guidance. Seek His direction for your life and work. You can trust that God knows the job market and more than that, He knows you. Together you'll find a solution to financial woes and the light of hope will come back into your life. Surrender your money miseries and seek first the Kingdom. You might be surprised at how quickly things will turn around.

Do your work willingly, as though you were serving the Lord himself.

Colossians 3:23 CEV

"Come to me, all you who are weary and burdened, and I will give you rest."

Matthew 11:28 NIV

And we know that all things work together for good to those who love God, to those who are called according to His purpose.

Romans 8:28 NKJV

I can do everything through him who gives me strength.

Philippians 4:13 NIV

The Lord knows what is in everyone's mind. He understands everything you think. If you go to him for help, you will get an answer.

1 Chronicles 28:9 NCV

If you can't excel with talent, triumph with effort.

Dave Weinbaum

Advice from Abraham Lincoln

You cannot bring about prosperity by
    discouraging thrift.

You cannot strengthen the weak by weakening
    the strong.

You cannot help the wage earner by pulling down
    the wage payer.

You cannot help the poor by destroying the rich.

You cannot establish sound security on borrowed
    money.

You cannot keep out of trouble by spending more
    than you earn.

Hope and a Prayer

Lord, as economic forces change in the world, many jobs have been lost and many talented and devoted workers find themselves without income to meet the needs of their families. Please be with each person who seeks the best possibilities for future growth and happiness. Bless each one with showers of opportunities and generous seeds of hope. You know the life purpose of each of your children. Guide those in need of new income to your endless resources.

Amen

Five: Is Anything Really that Important?

It's not very pleasant in my corner of the world at three o'clock in the morning. But for people who like cold, wet, ugly bits it is something rather special.

Eeyore, A.A.Milne

Sometimes the losses we endure in life can leave us with a feeling that perhaps nothing is really that important. Depressed thoughts enter our hearts and minds and before we know it, we struggle to find reasons to get up in the morning. Somewhat like the author of the book in the Bible called, Ecclesiastes we start to feel like there's nothing new under the sun and that we're just chasing the wind.

The problem with a "nothing matters" perspective is that life feels meaningless and all your seeds of hope dry up, leaving you parched and thirsty, but you don't know why. Soon your perception of the world is colored by your negative attitude and you may even wonder why you were born.

How can you shake this kind of mindset? Move to higher ground! Look up and look around. Strive for an attitude adjustment in every area of your life. Helen Keller said, "No pessimist ever discovered the secrets of the stars or sailed to an uncharted land or opened a new heaven to the human spirit." Seek out the people in your life who always carry an attitude of hope, who have such an abundance of it they are willing to give some to you.

Align yourself with those who can refresh your spirit and fertilize your dormant landscape with new seeds of hope. The challenges of life can certainly keep you reeling and wondering what really matters. The fact is that you matter. You matter so much that the God of the Universe actually sent His only Son to this planet just to be sure you would make it safely back to heaven someday. Everything about you matters to God and to the people who love you on earth as well.

It's time to awaken new hopes and dreams!

People harvest only what they plant. If they plant to satisfy their sinful selves, their sinful selves will bring them ruin. But if they plant to please the Spirit, they will receive eternal life from the Spirit. We must not become tired of doing good. We will receive our harvest of eternal life at the right time if we do not give up.

Galatians 6:7-9 NCV

Summing it all up, friends, I'd say you'll do best by filling your minds and meditating on things true, noble, reputable, authentic, compelling, gracious—the best, not the worst; the beautiful, not the ugly; things to praise, not things to curse.

Philippians 4:8 The Message

Those who wait for perfect weather will never plant seeds; those who look at every cloud will never harvest crops.

Ecclesiastes 11:4 NCV

Cast your bread upon the waters,
For you will find it after many days.

Ecclesiastes 11:1 NKJV

A happy person is not a person in a certain set of circumstances, but rather a person with a certain set of attitudes.

Hugh Downs

The creation of a thousand forests is in one acorn.

Ralph Waldo Emerson

Any fact facing us is not as important as our attitude toward it, for that determines our success or failure.

Norman Vincent Peale

The longer I live the more I realize the impact of attitude on life. Attitude to me is more important than the past, than education, than money, than circumstances, than failures, than success, than what others think, or say, or do. I am convinced that life is 10% what happens to me and 90% how I react to it.

Chuck Swindoll

Hope and a Prayer

Lord, when we wonder whether anything in this life is important, please help us change our direction. Help us to think about things that remind us of your goodness and of the possibilities that exist all around us. Remind us that an attitude adjustment may be as simple as starting the day with a prayer and a smile. Comfort us when we lose hope in ourselves and draw us close enough to you, to breathe in a new perspective and a new attitude.

AMEN

Attitude Adjustments

Complain about the rain--or rejoice that the grass

is getting watered for free

Be sad about what I lack--

or be grateful for what I have

Grumble that I'm lame, or be grateful I can walk

Blame my parents for what I missed, or praise

them that I exist

See the thorns, or love the roses

Be bitter and lonely, or seek new friends

Whine about my job, or be grateful I have a job

See the worst or hope for the best...

What kind of day will you choose?

The Seeds of Healthy Living

❧

Seize life! Eat bread with gusto,

Drink wine with a robust heart.

Oh yes—God takes pleasure in your pleasure!

Dress festively every morning.

Don't skimp on colors and scarves.

Relish life with the spouse you love

Each and every day of your precarious life.

Each day is God's gift.

Ecclesiastes 9:7-9 The Message

Prayer of Hope for Today

Lord, each day we awaken to a new sunrise we have the opportunity to draw closer to You. Each breath, gives us little moments to enjoy: a fresh cup of coffee, a bird singing outside the window, a beautiful cloudless sky. It doesn't take a lot to bring us an awareness of Your Presence. Your stamp is on all things. You know how important healthy minds and hearts and bodies are to achieving Your purposes in the world. Thank You for providing for all we need to make that possible. Thank You for healing us when we aren't well. We rejoice in You.

AMEN

One: The Dreaded Diagnosis!

> There is no medicine like hope, no incentive so great, and no tonic so powerful as expectation of something tomorrow.
>
> *Orison Swett Marden*

God knows everything about us! He knows what we need and that we're going to need Him even before we do. When you face the difficult news of serious illness, the kind that touches your mortality and makes you gulp hard, He's there.

If you've received news that something in your body is no longer working as it should, you may wonder where you can find real hope. After all, can hope change anything, or can it make you better in any way?

Amazingly, the answer is yes. Hope, the kind that has been rooted in your soul comes quickly to your aid, rising to the top of your thoughts and pushing against your fears. Hope remembers that you are still the same wonderful you no matter what your body does. Hope provides optimism, a more cheerful outlook and strength for your spirit.

As hard as it is to receive news of serious or even terminal illness, the truth is that God is with you every step of the way. The One who created you and who knows you intimately walks with you, holding you in his arms for safe keeping. You always have hope in Him no matter what life brings your way.

You are God's child; always have been, always will be. Rest in His love and look to Him to inspire your heart and mind over the next weeks and months and years of your life. You and He are in this together. May He shine His light on your life and on your health today.

You that are near despair, let this be the strength that nerves your arm and steels your heart. "Jesus Christ of the seed of David was raised from the dead according to Paul's gospel."

C.H. Spurgeon

Still, I know that God lives—the One who gives me back my life—and eventually he'll take his stand on earth.

Job 19:26 The Message

But he took our suffering on him and felt our pain for us. We saw his suffering and thought God was punishing him. But he was wounded for the wrong we did; he was crushed for the evil we did. The punishment, which made us well, was given to him, and we are healed because of his wounds.

Isaiah 53:4-5 NCV

Heal me, O Lord, and I shall be healed; Save me, and I shall be saved, For You are my praise.

Jeremiah 17:14 NKJV

Hope springs eternal in the human breast;
Man never is, but always to be blest
The soul, uneasy and confined from home,
Rests and expatiates in a life to come.

Alexander Pope

All human wisdom is summed up in two words —
wait and hope.

Alexander Dumas

The only disability in life is a bad attitude.

Scott Hamilton

A strong positive attitude will create more miracles
than any wonder drug.

Patricia Neal

You never know how much you really believe
anything until its truth or falsehood becomes a
matter of life and death to you.

C.S. Lewis

Hope and a Prayer

Lord, please be with Your people who deal
with the reality of failing health. Bless them
with courage and strength to see Your hand
at work even in their personal concerns and
situations. Walk beside them through every
doctor appointment and every step in the process
of caring for their illness. If possible, Lord, heal
them. In all cases, grant them Your continual
comfort and give them peace.

AMEN

Two: Caregivers... Offering the Heart of Hope

The most eloquent prayer is the prayer through hands that heal and bless. The highest form of worship is the worship of unselfish Christian service. The greatest form of praise is the sound of consecrated feet seeking out the lost and helpless.

Billy Graham

Standing head and shoulders above the rest of us are those who reach out in love and mercy to people who need continual care. Some do it as a profession, a choice to work each day to relieve the suffering of others. Others volunteer their services and give countless hours of care to those most in need. These are the caregivers of the world, the ones who help people maintain courage and dignity. They offer hope to those caught in the web of serious illness or limited mobility.

Caregivers are beacons of hope because they won't give up or turn their backs on those in need. They practice "love your neighbor" in the highest possible form. They are generous, giving people who need our prayers and support.

As you consider the caregivers you know, tending to the needs of a particular person or to groups of people, offer prayers to sustain them. Ask God to give them a spirit of joy even when they feel weary, and a heart of hope, even when they know hope is beyond reason. God is a God of miracles and no one knows when he may intervene.

If you are a caregiver, then thank you. May God bless you for your selfless acts of love and compassion. He adores you for your generous spirit.

But those who live to please the Spirit will harvest everlasting life from the Spirit. So don't get tired of doing what is good. Don't get discouraged and give up, for we will reap a harvest of blessing at the appropriate time. Whenever we have the opportunity, we should do good to everyone.

Galatians 6:7-10 NLT

Whoever makes himself humble will be made great.

Matthew 23:12 NCV

Make sure you don't take things for granted and go slack in working for the common good; share what you have with others. God takes particular pleasure in acts of worship—a different kind of "sacrifice"—that takes place in kitchen and workplace and on the streets.

Hebrews 13:16 The Message

Since you cannot do good to all, you are to pay special regard to those who, by the accidents of time, or place, or circumstances, are brought into closer connection with you.

Augustine of Hippo

How far that little candle throws his beams!
So shines a good deed in a weary world.

William Shakespeare

Giving is the secret to a healthy life. Not necessarily money, but whatever a person has of encouragement and sympathy and understanding.

John D. Rockefeller, Jr.

Let us touch the dying, the poor, the lonely and the unwanted according to the graces we have received and let us not be ashamed or slow to do the humble work.

Mother Teresa

Christ has no body now on earth but yours; yours are the only hands with which he can do his work, yours are the only feet with which he can go about the world, yours are the only eyes through which his compassion can shine forth upon a troubled world. Christ has no body now on earth but yours.

Teresa of Avila

Hope and a Prayer

Lord, thank You for the generous self-sacrifice
of those who give personal attention and care
to others. We thank You for those who open
their hearts and their hands to take care of
those in need. We thank You for the people who
choose every day to plant seeds of hope in their
communities. Help all of us to be more like them,
to be Your hands and feet in this world every day.

AMEN

Three: Hope for When Eternity Beckons

You will turn back into the dust of the earth again, But your spirit will return to God who gave it.

Ecclesiastes 12:7 NCV

Intellectually, we understand the concept of the cycle of life. We know that people and animals and all living things, at some point, cease to live. The difficult part is that we like beginnings a whole lot more than we like endings. Beginnings come with hope. Endings are not as clear to us. Whether we face our own mortality or that of loved ones, endings require faith.

Faith brings hope, the kind of hope that lasts for eternity. Jesus brought eternity. From the moment He was resurrected, He showed us how it was done. He showed us how God would take our bodies and change them into beautiful eternal bodies. He closed the door on death and despair forever and, like a friendly innkeeper, He has gone back to heaven so He could get our rooms ready. He's already there, the bill has been paid, and He's set for us to check in. It's a pretty clear path when we trust Him.

We know that we can trust Him because everything He ever said was true. He never lied to anyone. He always told the truth. Heaven awaits us and all we have to do to get there is believe in the truth of Jesus. Eternity waits at Earth's finish line. Once we cross over we discover that we're in first place, that we won the prize. We are awarded one fabulous trip through heaven and that will take forever to complete. We have hope.

When eternity beckons, it gives us good reason to celebrate. We celebrate the lives of those we've loved. We celebrate their goodness and kindness and achievements. We celebrate the hard work they put into living and all they did to make the people around them happier. If we send them off with the kind of fireworks we might see on the 4th of July, we can be sure that as they arrive in heaven a beautiful reception awaits them there. It's a gloriously hopeful thing when we know we move from life to life eternal.

Pursue a righteous life—a life of wonder, faith, love, steadiness, courtesy. Run hard and fast in the faith. Seize the eternal life, the life you were called to, the life you so fervently embraced in the presence of so many witnesses.

1 Timothy 6:11-12 The Message

Jesus said, "Don't let your hearts be troubled. Trust in God, and trust in me. There are many rooms in my Father's house. I would not tell you this if it were not true. I am going there to prepare a place for you. After I go and prepare a place for you, I will come back and take you to be with me so that you may be where I am."

John 14:1-3 NCV

Jesus said to her, "I am the resurrection and the life. He who believes in Me, though he may die, he shall live. And whoever lives and believes in Me shall never die."

John 11:25-26 NKJV

And this world is fading away, along with everything it craves. But if you do the will of God, you will live forever.

1 John 2:17 NLT

So softly death succeeded life in her,
She did but dream of heaven, and she was there.

John Dryden

I came from God, and I'm going back to God, and I won't have any gaps of death in the middle of my life.

George MacDonald

Until our Master summons us, not a hair on our head can perish, not a moment of our life can be snatched from us. When He sends for us, it should seem but the message that the child is wanted at home.

Anthony Thorold

Eternity is the place where questions and answers become one.

Eli Wiesel

Hope and a Prayer

Father, we thank You that life continues. We thank You that You have not only provided an earthly home for us in our visit here, but that You've provided a heavenly home when this journey is over. We put our love, our trust, and our faith in You. We thank You for each person who has shared this journey with us and thank You that You'll be there to welcome each of us through Heaven's gate. Our lives are in Your hands. You are our hope and salvation.

AMEN

Four: Disabled, Enabled, Abled... Children of Hope

Love never gives up.
Love cares more for others than for self.
Love doesn't want what it doesn't have.

1 Corinthians 13:8 The Message

When a child is born, a mother and a father are born too. The role of being a parent is mixed with incredible emotions of joy and wonder, and fear and concern. Even the world view changes as new parents seek to understand how to love and nurture this little being who has come into their lives. How can they prepare this child for the world?

As monumental as that job is when you have a totally healthy child, it's even more difficult when your child is born with a physical or emotional or mental challenge. This child has a different set of rules and it's not always easy to learn those rules. At times, it can be hard to maintain a sense of hope.

When your child has special needs, you can be sure God knew you would be a special parent. He knew that you would take on the challenge with strength and love and that you would be extraordinary in your efforts to give your child the best possible life.

God sees how hard you try every day to give all you can to the welfare of your precious child. He knows you need help. He knows you need rest and He wants to offer you a peaceful place to draw near to Him.

You can pin your hopes on Him. He sees your heart and hears your prayers. May His presence and comfort guide your heart and mind as you strive to be the best parent you can be.

Children are a gift from the Lord; they are a reward from him.

Psalm 127:3 NLT

O, Lord, do good to those who are good, whose hearts are in tune with you.

Psalm 125:4 NLT

Some people brought their little children to Jesus so he could touch them, but his followers told them to stop. When Jesus saw this, he was upset and said to them, "Let the little children come to me. Don't stop them, because the kingdom of God belongs to people who are like these children. I tell you the truth, you must accept the kingdom of God as if you were a little child, or you will never enter it." Then Jesus took the children in his arms, put his hands on them, and blessed them.

Mark 10:13-16 NCV

Train up a child in the way he should go,
And when he is old he will not depart from it.

Proverbs 22:6 NKJV

He has achieved success who has loved much, laughed often and been an inspiration to little children.

Bessie Anderson Stanley

We can't form our children on our own concepts; we must take them and love them as God gives them to us.

Goethe

Hope and a Prayer

Lord, thank You for the blessing of children.
Thank You for creating them with intention,
with a plan for their good. Help us when we
feel weary, when the challenge of caring for
their particular needs feels like more than we
can bear. Give us a shoulder to lean on and a
place to rest and be renewed. Grant that those
who could help us would open their hearts
to us. Keep all of us close to You and give us
strength to be loving parents.

AMEN

We begin by imagining that we are giving to them;
we end by realizing that they have enriched us.

Pope John Paul II

The potential possibilities of any child are the most
intriguing and stimulating in all creation.

Ray L. Wilbur

The strongest principle of growth lies
in the human choice.

George Eliot

The mother eagle teaches her little ones to fly
by making their nest so uncomfortable that they
are forced to leave it and commit themselves
to the unknown world of air outside. And just so
does our God to us.

Hannah Whitall Smith

Five: *Those Senior Years*

"So, Lord, what hope do I have?" You are my hope.

Psalm 39:7 NCV

You may remember listening to your grandparents when you were young. They were probably talking about their aches and pains and how hard it was to get around. It may have seemed to you like they were speaking a foreign language. You couldn't imagine feeling like that.

Suddenly, you find the years have flown, fast forwarded you to being the older generation. Now you're the one with health issues, the one who can't get around quite as easily, the one faced with your own mortality.

What does God expect from you now? What do you expect from God? No matter how gray your hair might be, God always sees you as His child. He sees your potential and possibilities until the day He calls you to come home. He's on your side every step of the way, even when you don't walk as fast as you did thirty years ago.

The gift of aging is the one called life, the one where you have had the opportunity to grow in awareness and wisdom. You have learned things that others need to know and God gives you the chance to share those things.

He has walked with you a number of years now. He will continue to walk with you always. He knows how hard you've worked and how much you've tried to live in His grace. In light of His love, you have hope eternal. In light of the present, you have so much yet to give. Share your hope with those around you now. It will strengthen your heart and soul. That's a promise!

You got me when I was an unformed youth, God, and taught me everything I know. Now I'm telling the world your wonders; I'll keep at it until I'm old and gray.

Psalm 71:17-18 The Message

So teach us to number our days,
That we may gain a heart of wisdom.

Psalm 90:12 NKJV

Gray hair is like a crown of honor; it is earned by living a good life.

Proverbs 16:31 NCV

I created you and have cared for you since before you were born. I will be your God throughout your lifetime — until your hair is white with age. I made you, and I will care for you. I will carry you along and save you.

Isaiah 46:4 NLT

Though our bodies are dying, our spirits are being renewed every day. For our present troubles are quite small and won't last very long. Yet they produce for us an immeasurably great glory that will last forever!

2 Corinthians 4:16-17 NLT

The value of life lies not in the length of days, but in the use we make of them.

Montaigne

You will support us both when little and even to gray hairs.

Augustine of Hippo

He who counts the stars and calls them by their names, is in no danger of forgetting His own children. He knows your case as thoroughly as if you were the only creature He ever made, or the only saint He ever loved.

C.H.Spurgeon

Age, health, and stage in life have nothing to do with serving or not serving. In each season of life there are attributes and qualities of life and experience that God values in service.

Bruce Kemper

Hope and a Prayer

Lord, it's not always easy to face the simple fact of aging. When we're young, we can't picture it ever really happening to us. As we grow older, we try to adjust with each stage, each loss. Grant us grace as we age to accept the changes in our bodies, our minds, and our spirits. Keep us as healthy as possible and guide us until we are safely home with You again. We know that at any age, our real hope always rests in You.

AMEN

The Age of Grace

It is grace at the beginning,
and grace at the end. So that when you
and I come to lie upon our death beds,
the one thing that should comfort
and help and strengthen us there
is the thing that helped us in the beginning.
Not what we have been,
not what we have done,
but the grace of God in Jesus Christ our Lord.
The Christian life starts with grace,
it must continue with grace, it ends with grace.
Grace wondrous grace. By the grace of God I am
what I am. Yet not I,
but the grace of God which was with me.

D. Martyn Lloyd-Jones

SECTION FIVE:

The Miraculous Seeds of Faith

Faith means being sure of the things we hope for and
knowing that something is real even if we do not see it.
Faith is the reason we remember great people who lived in
the past. It is by faith we understand that the whole world
was made by God's command so what we see was made by
something that cannot be seen.

Hebrews 11:1-3 NCV

Prayer of Hope for Today

Father, we are slowly but surely learning what
it means to have faith in You. We are waking up
to the truths of the Spirit and how those things
affect our everyday lives. We are learning to trust
You and to have confidence in You. You placed
a seed of faith in us, planted in our hearts even
before we were born so that we could come to
know You. You invited us into life and You are
with us through all that we experience. We thank
You now for giving us a measure of Yourself so
that we can come to You and love You and share
this beautiful concept known as faith. Grant us
more faith each day we live.

AMEN

One: *When Faith Does Not Take Root*

> "So listen to the meaning of the story about the farmer. What is the seed that fell by the road? That seed is like the person who hears the message about the kingdom but does not understand it. The Evil One comes and takes away what was planted in that person's heart."
>
> *Matthew 13:18-19 NCV*

Have you ever felt lost? We're not talking about getting lost trying to find an address or wandering the aisles of a new mall, but feeling you've lost your sense of purpose or life direction. Actually, we're talking even more than that, because what's lost is your sense of connection to God, your faith.

When you were younger, you went along with the idea of faith because it was part of your family culture. You just went to church on Sunday though it didn't mean all that much to you. The good seed was planted, but you weren't ready for it. You weren't able to grasp it in a way that made sense for your life, so you allowed it to slip away.

As you grew older, you may have become convinced that matters of faith were intellectually beneath you, that things of God were really for children. Then something happens. Something shifts in your thinking and you start to wonder again whether any of that stuff you learned years ago could actually be grounded in truth.

You start to ask more questions and to realize that even though your faith did not take root in a noticeable way when you were younger, that perhaps something did happen. God's message, His voice was a seed planted within you, ready to take root and bloom in your life. All you have to do now is nurture it, fertilize it with prayer and prepare to grow in His love. Let no one steal the good seed of faith from you.

"I tell you the truth, you must accept the kingdom of God as if you were a little child, or you will never enter it. Then Jesus took the children in his arms, put his hands on them, and blessed them."

Mark 10:15-16 NCV

God's wisdom is something mysterious that goes deep into the interior of his purposes. You don't find it lying around on the surface. It's not the latest message, but more like the oldest—what God determined as the way to bring out his best in us, long before we ever arrived on the scene.

1 Corinthians 2:8-10 The Message

But we are not those who turn back and are lost. We are people who have faith and are saved.

Hebrews 10:39 NCV

You could just as well expect a plant to grow without air and water as to expect your heart to grow without prayer and faith.

C.H. Spurgeon

We seldom lose faith by a blow out, usually it is just a slow leak.

Unknown author

A little faith will bring your soul to heaven, but a lot of faith will bring heaven to your soul.

Dwight L. Moody

Do not seek to understand in order that you may believe, but believe so that you may understand.

Augustine of Hippo

The seed that is sown is scattered with an open hand. The sower in order to have a harvest has to turn loose the seed. He can't grip it in his fist; he can't hesitate to let it go; he can't just sprinkle a little bit here and there—he's got to generously sow it, he's got to let it go and let it go liberally, if he expects to have a great harvest. If he sows sparingly, that's the way he's going to reap; if he sows liberally and bountifully, that's the way his harvest is going to be.

C.H.Spurgeon

Hope and a Prayer

Lord, I know that my faith is small, that it is a little seedling and has not yet begun to bloom in the ways You desire. Thank You for planting Your seeds of faith within me. Even though I haven't always understood them, I thank You too for all the people who share their faith so that people like me can grow and blossom. Thank You for finding me when I lost my way. Help me to stay close to You and grow stronger in my faith and understanding of You.

Amen

Two: *Grown Up Faith*

When I was a child, I spoke and thought and reasoned as a child does. But when I grew up, I put away childish things. Now we see things imperfectly as in a poor mirror, but then we will see everything with perfect clarity. All that I know now is partial and incomplete, but then I will know everything completely, just as God knows me now. There are three things that will endure—faith, hope, and love—and the greatest of these is love.

1 Corinthians 13:11-13 NLT

The beautiful part of our faith is that it is always subject to growth. We may have greater faith in certain matters than we do in others. We may truly believe God has a plan and purpose for us, but still doubt that we'll figure out what it is. Or we may believe that God sees us and knows us sometimes, but not all the time. That's because our faith walks hand in hand with doubt. Our faith takes a long time to mature. We are always growing.

Consider the rest of the parable about the seed of the farmer from Matthew 13. When the soil was not fertilized, the seed died. When the soil was too rocky, the roots did not go deep enough and nothing could grow. When the soil was thorny, the seeds got choked in the weeds. It was only when the seeds were planted in prepared soil that they began to grow.

Your heart is the good soil. Your heart is the place where God plants his seeds of faith, hope, and love. He wants to bring more joy to your life, more possibility to your days, and more opportunity for you to know Him in a real and personal way. God wants you to know how great His love really is. He is the farmer. He offers seeds of faith and hope and love so that you can grow up strong and firm in Him. The One who provides you with air and water and light and food, is the same One who offers you His bounty through faith. He will harvest a great relationship with you, because He knows your heart is ready for Him.

But the godly will flourish like palm trees and grow strong like the cedars of Lebanon. For they are transplanted into the Lord's own house. They flourish in the courts of our God. Even in old age they will still produce fruit; they will remain vital and green.

Psalm 92:12-14 NLT

If you don't take your stand in faith, you will not have a leg to stand on.

Isaiah 7:9 The Message

For we walk by faith, not by sight.

2 Corinthians 5:7 NKJV

Without faith no one can please God. Anyone who comes to God must believe that he is real and that he rewards those who truly want to find him.

Hebrews 11:6 NCV

There is no love without hope, no hope without love, and neither hope nor love without faith.

Augustine of Hippo

The fruit of our faith is the fulfillment of our hope.

Diane Benze

God does not keep an extra supply of goodness that is higher than faith, and there is no help at all in anything that is below it. Within faith is where the Lord wants us to stay.

Julian of Norwich

Faith is from God, not from man. Man can do nothing to earn or receive it. We are right with God by faith alone.

Martin Luther

A living faith is not something you have to carry, but something that carries you.

J. H. Oldham

Hope and a Prayer

Lord, You have given us this incredible gift
called faith. Like children, we are not always
aware of how much we depend on You, or how
much faith provides the way for us to go, but
we are truly grateful to You. Help us to grow
up and become adults strong in our faith, eager
to embrace even more faith in every area of our
lives. We thank You for Your love even when
we can't feel it, for the hope You bring even
when we have lost our way, and for the faith that
sustains us through all things.

Amen

Three: *Prayer Matters*

One writer said this about prayer: "A prayer warrior is a person who is convinced that God is omnipotent—that God has the power to do anything, to change anyone, and to intervene in any circumstance. A person who truly believes this refuses to doubt God."

We may not consider ourselves to be "prayer warriors," but at the same time, we might realize that prayer matters. Something about prayer helps. It may be the first thing we do when life hands us an unexpected crisis, or it may be the last resort when we've tried to do everything ourselves to fix the problems. Either way, God is there, ready and willing to help. All He wants from us is that we would ask for His help.

Sometimes we aren't sure how to pray. We wonder if a prayer is just as effective when we're on our knees as when we're driving in the car. We wonder if there are people who are closer to God, who get more of their prayers answered, than we might. We like to think prayer really changes things, but when we're new at it, we're not sure.

The truth is that prayer is a gift to us. It's the word we use to describe God's invitation and opportunity for us to talk with Him. He wanted to make it easy. Every thought that we lift up to Him becomes part of our communication, part of our experience to have more of God in our everyday lives.

God desires a strong relationship with us because He loves us unconditionally. When we pray, we give Him the chance to help us with anything that concerns us. We let Him know through prayer that we value His help and His direction for our lives. Yes, prayer matters and it's a continual outgrowth of faith. Keep praying!

Anyone who is having troubles should pray. Anyone who is happy should sing praises. Anyone who is sick should call the church's elders. They should pray for and pour oil on the person in the name of the Lord. And the prayer that is said with faith will make the person well; the Lord will heal that person. And if that person has sinned, the sins will be forgiven. Confess your sins to each other and pray for each other so God can heal you. When a believing person prays, great things happen.

James 5:13-16 NCV

So Jesus answered and said to them, "Have faith in God. For assuredly, I say to you, whoever says to this mountain, 'Be removed and be cast into the sea,' and does not doubt in his heart, but believes those things he says will be done, he will have whatever he says. Therefore, I say to you, whatever things you ask when you pray, believe that you receive them, and you will have them."

Mark 11:22-24 NKJV

Keep on asking, and you will be given what you ask for. Keep on looking, and you will find. Keep on knocking, and the door will be opened. For everyone who asks, receives. Everyone who seeks, finds. And the door is opened to everyone who knocks.

Matthew 7:7-8 NLT

What can be more excellent than prayer; what is more profitable to our life; what sweeter to our souls; what more sublime, in the course of our whole life, than the practice of prayer!

Augustine of Hippo

Prayer opens the heart to God, and it is the means by which the soul, though empty, is filled by God.

John Bunyan

Heaven is full of answers to prayers for which no one ever bothered to ask.

Billy Graham

When Luther's puppy happened to be at the table, he looked for a morsel from the master, and watched with open mouth and motionless eyes. Luther said, "Oh, if I could only pray the way this dog watches the meat! All his thoughts are concentrated on the piece of meat. Otherwise, he has no thought, wish, or hope."

Martin Luther

Pray, and let God worry.

Martin Luther

Hope and a Prayer

Lord, it is hard for us to comprehend the beauty and the value of prayer. Here we are simple human beings in direct communication with the God of the Universe, You, the One who created all things. We are grateful that You are willing to hear our prayers and to give us strength and peace. We thank You that You keep us from experiencing untold difficulties simply because of Your love for us. Help us to turn to You, to rest at Your feet, and to share our hearts with You for all that we need. Help us to fully understand what a great friend we have in You.

Amen

Four: *Pulling Up the Weeds of Doubt*

> Faith given back to us after a night of doubt is a stronger thing, and far more valuable to us than faith that has never been tested.
>
> *Elizabeth Goudge*

Growing in faith feels good. You can actually feel the light of God's love on your face, much like the sunshine on a beautiful day. You can feel God's presence in the breeze as you walk along and witness His Spirit in every blade of grass. Life is good.

Then unexpectedly, something creeps into your heart and mind that you did not invite. It shows up and begins to question everything you've been enjoying. It causes you to wonder if you really did feel the breeze or the warmth of the sun on your face. That uninvited guest is doubt.

Doubt has always lingered behind faith, doing its best to disturb the calming influence and sense of peace faith brings. Doubt can attack those things that you've held dear for years, things you thought you believed so thoroughly that nothing could shake them. Yet life brings tragedy and drama. It brings crisis and illness and death and those things may cause fear, and fear brings doubt.

The best thing to remember is that doubt is a lie, pure and simple. It's the snake in the grass in the Garden of Eden, the heckler of truth. When doubt comes in, it's time to grab it squarely by its thorny stems and uproot it quickly. It may serve as a test for your faith but will never give you peace. It will never shine a light to guide your life. The best thing doubt can do is remind you how important your faith really is. Fertilize your faith, not your doubts.

So Peter went over the side of the boat and walked on the water toward Jesus. But when he looked around at the high waves, he was terrified and began to sink. "Save me, Lord!" he shouted.

Instantly Jesus reached out his hand and grabbed him. "You don't have much faith," Jesus said. "Why did you doubt me?" And when they climbed back into the boat, the wind stopped.

Matthew 14:29-32 NLT

Then he focused his attention on Thomas. "Take your finger and examine my hands. Take your hand and stick it in my side. Don't be unbelieving. Believe."

Thomas said, "My Master! My God!"

Jesus said, "So, you believe because you've seen with your own eyes. Even better blessings are in store for those who believe without seeing."

John 20:27-29 The Message

Doubt sees the obstacles,
Faith sees the way.
Doubt sees the darkest night,
Faith sees the day.
Doubt dreads to take a step,
Faith soars on high.
Doubt questions, "Who believes?"
Faith answers, "I!"

Author Unknown

Feed your faith and starve your doubts to death.

Andrew Murray

Too often we forget that the great men of faith reached the heights they did only by going through the depths.

Os Guinness

Faith lives in honest doubt.

Tennyson

Doubt isn't the opposite of faith; it is an element of faith.

Paul Tillich

Where do you live? Many a believer lives in the "cottage of doubt," when he might be living in the "mansion of faith."

C.H.Spurgeon

Hope and a Prayer

Lord, you are most gracious and kind to us. You stick by us even when we are mired in doubt. You wait for us to see Your light and to walk back to You, knowing that we cannot spend much time apart from You and be happy. Help us weed the doubts that keep us from being wholly faithful and available to hear You, see You, and love You.

AMEN

Five: *Faith and Trust, You and God!*

Trust the past to God's mercy, the present to God's love, and the future to God's providence.

Augustine of Hippo

Perhaps we find it difficult in our current culture to trust God because we've lost so much faith and trust in the people and the things around us. Ideals that we once took for granted, like the innocence of childhood or the joy of living in a family, seem lost. Occupational loyalty, social security, people in ministry; none of these seem to have the trusted value they once did. They leave us feeling uncertain as to what we can really believe. What do we do? What or who can we really trust?

The one thing that has never changed is God. God has not stopped caring about us. He has never ceased to believe in our ultimate possibilities to be better human beings. God wants us to have faith not only in the belief that He will come back someday, but to trust that He is in control right now and that He holds tomorrow in His hand.

God calls us to trust Him. He wants us to open our hearts and know that He is our cornerstone, our true foundation of trust. He is our certainty even in the midst of mind-boggling changes all around us.

Consider the things you have placed your faith and your trust in and see if God is at the top of your list. If not, why not? Only He will not disappoint you. Only His faithfulness endures forever.

But let everyone who trusts in you be happy; let them sing glad songs forever.

Psalm 5:11 NCV

The Lord is my rock and my fortress and my
    deliverer;
My God, my strength, in whom I will trust.

Psalm 18:2 NKJV

All I have seen teaches me to trust the Creator for all I have not seen.

Emerson

Trust the Lord and do good,
Live in the land and feed on truth.
Enjoy serving the Lord,
   and he will give you what you want.
Depend on the Lord;
Trust him, and he will take care of you.
Then your goodness will shine like the sun,
and your fairness like the noonday sun.

Psalm 37:3-6 NCV

Cursed is the strong one who depends on mere humans, Who thinks he can make it on muscle alone and sets God aside as dead weight. He's like a tumbleweed on the prairie, out of touch with the good earth. He lives rootless and aimless in a land where nothing grows.

But blessed is the man who trusts me, God, the woman who sticks with God. They're like trees replanted in Eden, putting down roots near the rivers—Never a worry through the hottest of summers, never dropping a leaf, Serene and calm through droughts, bearing fresh fruit every season.

Jeremiah 17:5-8 The Message

Quit swearing, quit wrestling. It is not TRY but TRUST.

John G. Lake

Even if I knew that tomorrow the world would go to pieces, I would still plant my apple tree.

Martin Luther

Trust in yourself and you are doomed to
    disappointment.
Trust in your friends and they will die and leave
    you.
Trust in money and you may have it taken away
    from you.
Trust in reputation and some slanderous tongues
    will blast it.
But trust in God and you are never to be
    confounded in time or in eternity.

Dwight Moody

Hope and a Prayer

Lord, teach us to trust You in all things, for all things, and through all things. We are fragile and easily rattled. We are uncertain of our steps, uneasy in crowds, afraid to look each other in the eye. We have misplaced and misused the trust we once knew. Guide us to be discerning enough to know the people and the ideas and the places where we can give our trust. Help us to trust that You are working for our good in all things as long as we place our confidence in You.

Amen

Learning to Trust God

Do not look forward to the changes
and chances of this life in fear; look to them
with full hope that, as they arise, God,
whose you are, will deliver you out of them.
He is your keeper. He has kept you hitherto.
Do you but hold fast to his dear hand,
and he will lead you safely through all things;
and, when you cannot stand, he will
bear you in his arms. Do not look forward
to what may happen tomorrow.
Our Father will either shield you
from suffering, or he will give you
strength to bear it.

FRANCIS DE SALES

Seeds of Hope for Unexpected Life Events

I have observed something else in this world of ours. The fastest runner doesn't always win the race, and the strongest warrior doesn't always win the battle. The wise are often poor, and the skillful are not necessarily wealthy. And those who are educated don't always lead successful lives. It is all decided by chance, by being at the right place at the right time. People can never predict when hard times might come. Like fish in a net or birds in a snare, people are often caught by sudden tragedy.

Ecclesiastes 9:11-12 NLT

Prayer of Hope for Today

Father in Heaven, we are at Your mercy. We know that we cannot change the course of events that You have planned. We cannot stop a hurricane from washing houses away, or a tornado from destroying our property. We cannot prevent accidental deaths or abusive situations. We can only do one thing. We can only put our lives in Your hands, appealing to Your protection and love to spare us from life's catastrophes. We come to You always with hope and faith, knowing that You seek our good. We thank You for Your continual love and mercy no matter what chance may bring our way. Watch over us and keep us close to You always.

AMEN

One: *When Bad News Strikes!*

> In all troubles you should seek God. You should not set him over against your troubles, but within them. God can only relieve your troubles if you in your anxiety cling to him. Trouble should not really be thought of as this thing or that in particular, for our whole life on earth involves trouble; and through the troubles of our earthly pilgrimage we find God.
>
> *Augustine of Hippo*

News headlines around the world are often full of mind-blowing tragedies. One story tells us of innocent children who are slain by a gunman for no apparent reason. Another article tells of people in a theatre who are shot to death by a man only to bring him a moment of national attention. We read on to discover a bomb has gone off in a local stadium and hundreds have been hospitalized or are left dead. The tragedies go on and on and such news puts a hole in the heart of every reader. The world doesn't make sense. Nothing feels safe, and everyone and every place is to be feared because the world seems out of control.

Where is the hope for our lives when we know we cannot even protect our own children, when we know we can't stop the madness? Our hope is right where it has always been. Our hope is in God. Hope comes from realizing that God knows those things that grieve us and He understands why we're overwhelmed with so much bad news. He does what He has always done, He reminds us of the Good News.

The Good News is the hope we have in Jesus. The Good News is that God has already made plans for those who trust Him and believe in Him. The Good News is that Jesus will come again and take His children to a new home where tragedy will not exist, where suffering will be no more.

Perhaps the best thing we can do after we read through the morning paper is to pick up God's Word and read through the Psalms or our favorite Bible passages. Seek God's comfort for each day, trusting that He watches over you and those you love.

Therefore let all the faithful pray to you while you may be found; surely the rising of the mighty waters will not reach them. You are my hiding place; you will protect me from trouble and surround me with songs of deliverance.

Psalm 32:6-7 NIV

For those who are evil will be destroyed, but those who hope in the Lord will inherit the land.

Psalm 37:9 NIV

Fix your thoughts on what is true and honorable and right. Think about things that are pure and lovely and admirable. Think about things that are excellent and worthy of praise. Keep putting into practice all you learned from me and heard from me and saw me doing, and the God of peace will be with you.

Philippians 4:8-9 NLT

Whatever sort of tribulation we suffer, we should always remember that its purpose is to make us spurn the present and reach out to the future.

John Calvin

In tribulation, immediately draw near to God with trust, and you will receive strength, enlightenment, and instruction.

John of the Cross

There are times when God asks nothing of His children except silence, patience, and tears.

Charles Seymour Robinson

God's people have no assurances that the dark experiences of life will be held at bay, much less that God will provide some sort of running commentary on the meaning of each day's allotment of confusion, boredom, pain, or achievement. It is no great matter where we are, provided we see that the Lord has placed us there, and that He is with us.

John Newton

We must face today as children of tomorrow. We must meet the uncertainties of this world with the certainty of the world to come.

A. W. Tozer

Hope and a Prayer

Lord, our hearts break with tragic news from the daily headlines. We don't understand how such cruelty can be part of the experience of living. All we know is that we must turn from the bad news and seek You, and the Good News to lift our spirits and keep us going on. The world is so much at our finger tips that we fill up with information about adversity everywhere. We are driven to our knees, to the only One who can do anything about such things. Watch over Your children, Lord, and keep them safe wherever they are.

AMEN

Two: And They Call Them "Acts of God!"

In the storm the tree strikes deeper roots in the soil, in the hurricane the inhabitants of the house abide within, and rejoice in its shelter. So by suffering the Father would lead us to enter more deeply into the love of Christ.

Andrew Murray

It's interesting that we call hurricanes, tsunamis, and earthquakes, "Acts of God!" Perhaps we label them as such because they are so big, so devastating in their impact that we recognize only God has such power. Maybe it's because we as humans don't want any part in the responsibility and the result of such huge storms and seismic events.

When Hurricane Sandy hit the Atlantic Coast in 2012, it became the deadliest and most costly storm in the United States since Katrina hit New Orleans. Tropical cyclones affected millions of people's lives and rebuilding costs billions of dollars. These natural disasters do a lot of damage, but they also remind us that as human beings we're all in this together. Petty grievances, racial differences, belief systems are no longer the big concern, because prayers are going up to God for help in every possible way.

As we begin to help each other clean up the messes of these huge storms, we begin to hope again. We see the opportunity to serve God in ways we hadn't recognized before. We see the chance to become God's hands and feet and heart to people in such dire need.

God shelters us from certain storms in life. He protects us more than we realize from many disasters, but when we're caught up in one, He is there too. He shows Himself in hundreds of ways through other people; some who feel called to donate, some who start prayer chains, and others who literally dig in and help clear away the debris. God's message is always hope.

Stay rooted in God, nurtured by His love, and rejoice in the shelter He provides to you each day. Give Him praise for His saving grace and protection, for He is your everlasting hope.

Praise God from earth,
You sea dragons, you fathomless ocean deeps;
Fire and hail, snow and ice,
Hurricanes obeying his orders…

Psalm 148:7-8 The Message

Praise God in His sanctuary;
Praise Him in His mighty firmament!
Praise Him for His mighty acts;
Praise Him according to His excellent greatness!

Psalm 150:1-2 NKJV

He gives strength to those who are tired and more power to those who are weak.

Isaiah 40:29 NCV

"For I was hungry and you fed me. I was thirsty, and you gave me drink. I was a stranger, and you invited me into your home. I was naked, and you gave me clothing. I was sick, and you cared for me. I was in prison, and you visited me."

Matthew 25:35-36 NLT

The only haven of safety is in the mercy of God, as manifested in Christ, in whom every part of our salvation is complete.

John Calvin

If we were logical, the future would be bleak indeed. But we are more than logical. We are human beings, and we have faith, and we have hope.

Jacques Cousteau

The future is as bright as the promises of God.

Adoniram Judson

Hope, like faith, is nothing if it is not courageous; it is nothing if it is not ridiculous.

Thornton Wilder

Hope and a Prayer

Lord, in this generation alone, all around the world, natural disasters have hit unsuspecting people, with costs that are too hard to bear. We pray that You will be with us when disasters strike so that we can be strong and help each other deal with the losses. Help us take care of each other when they occur. Open our hearts and our hands in service and give us reasons to always hope in You. We trust that in all things, You are with us, now and forever.

AMEN

Three: When You Feel Like that Guy in the Bible, Job!

> Why is life given to a man whose way is hidden, whom God has hedged in? For sighing has become my daily food; my groans pour out like water. What I feared has come upon me; what I dreaded has happened to me. I have no peace, no quietness; I have no rest, but only turmoil."
>
> *Job 3:23-26 NIV*

If you've ever had a series of setbacks that occurred in your life at the same time, you may have wondered if you would survive it all. The biblical story of Job describes a man who did everything he could to please God and yet calamity fell on him over and over again. He couldn't understand what was happening.

Some of our "Job" experiences happen for a few days and are gone, but other times, they take us on such a downward spiral that we wonder if recovery is possible. Worse yet, we wonder if God is going to help us get through it.

155

We wonder if God is punishing us or if there is yet hope for the future.

In some very real ways, Job's story is our story. We live on planet earth and that means we live on the battlefield between good and evil, between the God who loves and created us and Satan who wants to devour us. We know which side we want to be on when that battle is over, but we aren't always aware that we are continually being asked to choose whom we will serve. Temptations come, jobs are lost, marriages are destroyed, and all kinds of troubling things happen and the question always remains. What will our response be? How will we choose?

In the end, God restored everything to Job and gave him even more besides. In the end, He will do the same for us. We can't even imagine what good things He has in store for us in heaven, but we know He's already made plans for our good. Our job then is to keep choosing God. We have to hold on to all we know of Him and all we believe. We have to send Satan packing because He's the loser here and we don't want to play his game.

Whatever you're going through, remember your Creator. Remember the One who loves you more than it's even possible to realize. He's the One who sent His Son to the cross just for you. He's the One who has planned a future where there are no tears. Keep choosing Him!

The experts of our day haven't a clue about what this eternal plan is. If they had, they wouldn't have killed the Master of the God-designed life on a cross. That's why we have this Scripture text:

No one's ever seen or heard anything like this,
Never so much as imagined anything quite like it—
What God has arranged for those who love him.

1 Corinthians 2:8-9 The Message

So in Christ Jesus you are all children of God through faith.

Galatians 3:26 NIV

God's word is true,
and everything he does is right.
He loves what is right and fair;
the Lord's love fills the earth.

Psalm 33:4-5 NCV

The God who made the world and everything in it is the Lord of the land and the sky. He does not live in temples built by human hands. This God is the One who gives life, breath, and everything else to people.

Acts 17:24-25 NCV

Never be afraid to trust an unknown future to a known God.

Corrie ten Boom

God does not give us everything we want, but He does fulfill His promises...leading us along the best and straightest paths to Himself.

Dietrich Bonhoeffer

Godliness is glory in the seed, and glory is godliness in the flower.

William Gurnall

Our heavenly Father never takes anything from his children unless he means to give them something better.

George Muller

In his love, he clothes us, enfolds us and embraces us; that tender love completely surrounds us, never to leave us.

Julian of Norwich

There are two kinds of people: those who say to God, "Thy will be done," and those to whom God says, "All right, then, have it your way."

C.S Lewis

The will of God will never take you where the grace of God cannot keep you.

Unknown author

Hope and a Prayer

Dear Lord, No matter what things look like, no matter how difficult the path seems to us, we trust that You are truly aware of all of our circumstances. We believe in Your faithfulness and in Your incredible love for us. In all things, and in all ways, we put our lives before You and ask you to be our hope and our strength in every setback. We thank You for giving us the chance to keep choosing You.

AMEN

Four: Your Personal Roller Coaster: Hold On!

For each of us, life can feel like a roller coaster. One minute you're heading toward the top of the highest peak, somewhat apprehensive, but excited. The next minute you're heading downward faster than you ever thought you'd go and you're not sure if you're screaming with sheer terror or joy. What do you do? You hold on! You hold on to the hope that God always has for you.

Your roller coaster experience may be about crashing financial pictures, or about the unexpected death of someone you love, or that your spouse has been deployed to a volatile part of the world. Personal tragedies abound and somehow between the ones we experience ourselves and the ones we hear about from our friends, we're overwhelmed with those tragedies. We can hardly catch our breath before another one hits us. It's definitely not an easy ride.

How do we smooth things out and hold on? We find an anchor. We find a support system that is so strong we know that it cannot fall apart or fail us because it keeps us looking up and holding on. God gave us His Son and His Spirit to comfort us and strengthen us. He knows we'll hit hard times along with the good times, and so He never leaves us alone for even one second.

He sees you! He knows when your heart is broken or when your fears are mounting. He offers you His steady hand and He is ready even now to wrap you in His care. He calls out to you to be still, sit with Him, feel His Presence, and know that He is beside you in all the ups and downs. Hold on to Him in every twist and turn life takes and remember that He is still in control. His message is hope and peace.

O, Lord, you alone are my hope. I've trusted you, O Lord, from childhood. Yes, you have been with me from birth; from my mother's womb you have cared for me.

Psalm 71:5-6 NLT

God is our refuge and strength, an ever-present help in trouble. Therefore, we will not fear, though the earth give way and the mountains fall into the heart of the sea, though its waters roar and foam and the mountains quake with their singing.

Psalm 46:1-3 NIV

I pray that the God who gives hope will fill you with much joy and peace while you trust in him. Then your hope will overflow by the power of the Holy Spirit.

Romans 15:13 NCV

In God alone is there faithfulness and faith in the trust that we may hold to him, to his promise, and to his guidance. To hold to God is to rely on the fact that God is there for me, and to live in this certainty.

Karl Barth

All things are possible to him who believes, yet more to him who hopes, more still to him who loves, and most of all to him who practices and perseveres in these three virtues.

Brother Lawrence

It will greatly comfort you if you can see God's hand on your losses and your crosses.

C.H. Spurgeon

Faith puts Christ between itself and circumstances so that it cannot see them.

F.B.Meyer

I have experienced His presence in the deepest hell that man can create. I have really tested the promises of the Bible, and believe me, you can count on them.

Corrie ten Boom

Hope and a Prayer

Father, unexpected things happen. We aren't always prepared. We know that You are prepared though, and that You knew even before things happened what would come to be. We ask that You would help us to stay strong, to recognize Your loving hand in the midst of our struggles and our concerns and know that we can put our trust in You. Grant us Your peace and Your comfort and let us always hope in You for every circumstance of life.

AMEN

Five: *When You Need Hope and Justice!*

Injustice, swift, erect, and unconfined,
Sweeps the wide earth, and tramples o'er mankind.

Alexander Pope

We may not actually give a lot of thought to what justice is, until something happens where we suffer an injustice. We recognize injustice because it hides behind those things that seem like truths. Our legal system, though one of the best in the world, is one that sometimes leaves the victim with a new set of frustrations. It may be too costly to pursue justice, or the criminal may have been freed on a technicality. We might feel that the system will not work for us. We forget that we are human beings. Jesus recommended that we try to forgive each other and settle matters without having to take them to a court system. Once there, the courts have control and matters are taken out of our hands. One thing we know for sure, God is just. He digs deeper to discover the motives of the heart than any other system can do. He knows exactly who we are. Even when systems fail us,

He does not. He is an ever-faithful and ever-Present hope when we seek justice and fight for our cause. Ultimately, He will make certain that justice is served with love and mercy. We rest in that hope.

But I do nothing without consulting the Father. I judge as I am told. And my judgment is absolutely just, because it is according to the will of God who sent me; it is not merely my own.

John 5:30 (Jesus) NLT

Settle matters quickly with your adversary who is taking you to court. Do it while you are still together on the way, or your adversary may hand you over to the judge, and the judge may hand you over to the officer, and you may be thrown into prison.

Matthew 5:25 NIV

Whitewashing bad people and throwing mud on good people are equally abhorrent to God.

Proverbs 17:15 The Message

The Lord's eyes see everything; he watches both evil and good people.

Proverbs 15:3 NCV

True goodness forgets itself and goes out to do the right thing for no other reason than that it is right.

Lesslie Newbigin

I am not bound to win but I am bound to be true. I am not bound to succeed but I am bound to live up to what light I have. I must stand with anybody that stands right; stand with him while he is right and part with him when he goes wrong.

Abraham Lincoln

God is able to make a way out of no way and transform dark yesterdays into bright tomorrows. This is our hope for becoming better men and women. This is our mandate for seeking to make a better world.

Martin Luther King, Jr.

The Bible must be considered as the great source of all the truth by which men are to be guided in government as well as in all social transactions.

Noah Webster

The seed of God is in us. Given an intelligent and hard-working farmer, it will thrive and grow up to God, whose seed it is; and accordingly its fruits will be God-nature. Pear seeds grow into pear trees, nut seeds into nut trees, and God seed into more of the image of God.

Meister Eckhart (adapted)

Hope and a Prayer

Lord, we ask that You would stand with us when we face any kind of legal issues, when we ever have to appear in a court setting. We ask that You would bless us with fair minded people and good counsel, those who would hear the truths of our situation and help us take care of matters quickly. When we're wrong we ask forgiveness. When we're right we ask for Your protection and help and grace. We put our hope in You as the One source of truth and mercy.

AMEN

Little Seeds of Hope

If hope is truly a seed, it is one that is meant to be sown in all areas of life. We must trust in it when we cannot yet see any evidence that it is real. We must nurture it through wind and rain and storms of life, and water it in the sunshine.

Eventually, we'll begin to see it take shape. A fragile leaf will show itself, giving us momentary relief, blessing us with a sense that things are looking up. From there, the light of hope begins to grow and strengthen and push its way through all the darkness and the mire that we have known. It will show itself and renew us. It will blossom and grow.

God is that hope. When we cannot see Him or feel His Presence, He is at work planting more seeds so that we will discover Him on our pathway. When we are weak, He grows stronger, pushing us past those things that sap our energy. He pours out His great love like sunshine until hope bursts forth in us again to keep us going and growing in faith. One day, He will harvest those who have hoped in Him and bring everlasting joy.

Until then, be blessed by His grace and the little seeds of hope that you enjoy along the way. As Goethe, said:

"We must not hope to be mowers,

And to gather the ripe old ears,

Unless we have first been sowers

And watered the furrows with tears.

It is not just as we take it,

This mystical world of ours,

Life's field will yield as we make it

A harvest of thorns or flowers."

Things I hope for...

_____

_____

_____

_____

_____

_____

_____

_____

_____

_____

*If seeds in the black earth can turn into such beautiful
roses, what might not the heart of man become in its long
journey toward the stars?*

G.K. CHESTERTON

_____

Things I hope for...

_____

_____

_____

_____

_____

_____

_____

_____

_____

_____

A religious hope does not only bear up the mind under her sufferings, but makes her rejoice in them.

JOSEPH ADDISON

_____

Things I hope for...

_____

_____

_____

_____

_____

_____

_____

_____

_____

_____

_____

❧

*The word which God has written on the brows of all
mankind is hope.*

VICTOR HUGO (ADAPTED)

❧

Things I hope for...

_____

_____

_____

_____

_____

_____

_____

_____

_____

_____

*If we were logical, the future would be bleak, indeed. But
we are more than logical. We are human beings, and we
have faith, and we have hope, and we can work.*

JACQUES COUSTEAU

_____

Things I hope for...

_Every blade of grass, each leaf, each separate petal, is an
inscription speaking of hope._

RICHARD JEFFERIES

Things I hope for...

_____

_____

_____

_____

_____

_____

_____

_____

_____

_____

_____

Whatever enlarges hope will also exalt courage.
SAMUEL JOHNSON

_____

Things I hope for...

_____

_____

_____

_____

_____

_____

_____

_____

_____

_____

_____

*Far away there in the sunshine are my highest
aspirations. I may not reach them, but I can look up
and see their beauty, believe in them, and try to follow
where they lead.*

LOUISA MAY ALCOTT

_____

Things I hope for...

_____

_____

_____

_____

_____

_____

_____

_____

_____

_____

_____

Fear cannot be without hope nor hope without fear.
SPINOZA

Things I hope for...

_____

_____

_____

_____

_____

_____

_____

_____

_____

_____

_____

_____

_____

Hope is itself a species of happiness, and, perhaps, the chief happiness which this world affords.

SAMUEL JOHNSON

_____

Things I hope for...

_____

_____

_____

_____

_____

_____

_____

_____

_____

_____

*Hope is the pillar that holds up the world. Hope is the
dream of a waking man.*

PLINY THE ELDER

Things I hope for...

_____

_____

_____

_____

_____

_____

_____

_____

_____

_____

_____

Our ground of hope is that God does not weary of mankind.

RALPH W. SOCKMAN

_____

Things I hope for...

_____

_____

_____

_____

_____

_____

_____

_____

_____

_____

Believe in God with all your might, for hope rests on faith, love on hope, and victory on love.

NICHOLAS OF FLUE